Extremes

or

Balance?

by
Betty Miller

First Edition Published 1980
Second Printing 1982
Third Printing 1983
Fourth Printing 1984
Fifth Printing 1987
Sixth Printing 1988
Seventh Printing 1989
Eighth Printing 1991
Ninth Printing 1994
Tenth Printing 2003
Print On Demand

Extremes or Balance?

ISBN 1-57149-014-0

CHRIST UNLIMITED MINISTRIES, INC.
Pastor R.S. "Bud" Miller - Publisher
P.O. Box 850
Dewey, Arizona 86327
All Rights Reserved

Printed in U.S.A.

Scripture quotations are taken from the King James Version
unless otherwise indicated.

Contents

Preface

Greetings in the name of our Lord Jesus Christ:

I present this book to the body of Christ as the Holy Spirit presented it to me. I challenge you to allow God's Spirit of truth, and the Bible, to test the accuracy of the words within these pages. This book, part of the Overcoming Life Series, is also addressed to all seekers of truth who know not THE CHRIST UNLIMITED, as it would be my privilege to introduce you to Him.

During the early years of the ministry, I struggled to learn how to hear the voice of God. Once, while nervously waiting to speak before a large audience, and not being sure on what subject I should speak, I posed to the Lord in prayer this question: "Lord, what am I going to say to all these people?" In my spirit, I heard Him very clearly reply, "Betty, I was hoping you would not say anything, as I really wanted to speak." Yes, He wants to speak through us, as we yield to His Spirit. Submitting to the Lord and the guidance of the Holy Spirit, I found, was not only possible, but the only way He wants us to minister. **For it is not ye that speak, but the Spirit of your Father which speaketh in you (Matthew 10:20).**

This book is a gift from the Holy Spirit. I take no credit for it. If something within these pages blesses you, enlightens you, brings you closer to the Lord, releases you from fear or bondage, or heals or delivers you, then please lift your voice in praise to the precious Savior of our souls, Jesus Christ our Lord! On the other hand, if you find some of these things difficult to receive, hard to understand, or totally heretical from your viewpoint, would you also look to the Lord and ask Him if it could possibly be the truth? With an open and honest heart, will you ask God to change any pre-conceived ideas, and be free from traditions to receive of Him, His truth? His truth always brings freedom, never bondage. **And ye shall know the truth, and the truth shall make you free (John 8:32).**

In walking with the Lord, I have found we must obey the

things we feel He is speaking to us. In my personal life, I used to be fearful of speaking for the Lord because I was so afraid of missing Him and making mistakes. (He, of course, has now delivered me of all my fears. Praise Him!) He encouraged me not to quit because of mistakes when He spoke these words to me: "Betty, if I receive the glory and praise for all the things that are a blessing to people, I also receive the responsibility for your mistakes, as long as you are striving to please me. I am able to make even those work for your good." **And we know that all things work together for good to them that love God, to them who are the called according to his purpose (Romans 8:28).** We serve a wonderful, loving God, who encourages us to follow and obey Him that we might be blessed, and in turn bless others!

This book was written as an act of obedience to the Lord, whom I dearly love. I consider it an honor to write for Him. Years ago, when I was in prayer, the Lord spoke that I was to write a book, but I never felt it was God's timing, nor did I feel the unction or anointing to begin this work until now. Over the past year God has performed a series of miracles to confirm that it is now His time, and has made the arrangements for this to become a reality.

I pray that this book, along with the Overcoming Life Series, may help you learn to walk closer to our Lord, as He is THE CHRIST UNLIMITED!

I am, by His love,
A handmaiden of the Lord,

Betty Miller
February, 1980

If any man will do his will, he shall know of the doctrine, whether it be of God, or whether I speak of myself (John 7:17).

Foreword

It just seemed natural that I would do the foreword on this book since my wife, Betty, and myself, are "one flesh." God, through the Holy Spirit, has given by revelation to Betty many truths of His Word, which have been set forth in this book.

The Lord spoke to Betty about ten years ago that she was to write a book for Him, and that He would arrange the right time and place to write it. Betty simply took this vision and set it aside until God began to "quicken" her spirit to bring it forth. One morning, very early, Betty awakened, and began to write as the Lord dictated to her. In giving her this small initial portion of the book, He showed her how, by submitting to His Spirit, and completely yielding to Him, He would feed to her the message He wanted to share with the body of Christ. He also revealed how quickly and easily it would be completed. The messages that God has given in this Overcoming Life Series are to all who desire to become "overcomers" and be "conformed to the image of His son" (**Romans 8:29**). Our Lord is not satisfied that a person remains a "babe" in Christ, but longs for each "babe" to grow to maturity. He desires that we should strive to become overcomers, live the overcoming life, and claim the promises of the inheritance of all things that are to be given to the overcomers.

I thank God that He has allowed me to share such close love and companionship with Betty. I know that within her heart she has no personal ambitions, no personal ends to achieve. Betty has simply been doing the will of the Father in the writing of this anointed book. May the Lord bless you with this book, as He has blessed us in being a part of His work.

Yours in Christ,

Pastor R.S. "Bud" Miller

> **He that overcometh shall inherit all things; and I will be his God and he shall be my son (Revelation 21:7).**

Credits & Acknowledgments

ALL PRAISE AND CREDIT
GOES TO **THE CHRIST UNLIMITED**!

Truly Christ, the Father, and the Holy Spirit, are to be praised, not only for this book, but for our very lives. His sacrifice on Calvary made it possible to know Him and all the members of God's family.

As with the printing of any book, there are lots of people responsible for the words on these pages, physical words as well as spiritual words. All the people that have ever been a part of my life, all the people that have prayed and supported this ministry, my friends and my family have truly contributed to this work. Special credit should be given to my husband, Bud, whose faithful and loving prayers, encouragement, leadership, and love are a big part of this book. Also, to everyone whose books and articles I've read, to the ministers of the Gospel, whose sermons I've heard, I express my gratitude. For each has contributed, in some measure, to this book. The list is endless, but eternity has the records. So instead of naming individuals on this page and giving them earthly credit, I prefer the Lord Jesus Christ to reward them each as only He can. God bless you all, and may you be surprised as you open up the box that contains your heavenly treasures.

For the Son of man shall come in the glory of his Father with his angels; and then he shall reward every man according to his works (Matthew 16:27).

Introduction

EXTREMES OR BALANCE? is a book that looks at the many out-of-balance things that are going on in the Body of Christ in the light of God's Word. This book does not take a judgmental attitude toward individuals that promote these things but seeks to alert Christians to test and discern all things according to the Word of God.

Many Christians have hurt the cause of Christ through out-of-balance teachings and demonstrations. *EXTREMES OR BALANCE?* seeks to teach believers how to avoid those areas and walk in balance. This book deals with some of the more serious excesses and extremes in the Body of Christ.

EXTREMES OR BALANCE? gives believers the guidelines and help to be able to learn how to judge things without becoming judgmental. The Lord Himself warns us as Christians to **"...Beware of men" (Matthew 10:17).** All things done in the name of the Lord are not necessarily from Him. This book will help you to be discerning without being fearful or critical.

Extremes or Balance?

Proverbs 11:1: A false balance and unrighteous dealings are extremely offensive and shamefully sinful to the Lord, but a just weight is His delight (Amp.).

Extremes Bring Division

A pair of scales has always been representative of balance, justice and equity. The above verse in Proverbs tells us that when the balance is false it becomes sinful. Today many things have become "out-of-balance" in regard to the true teachings of the Bible; therefore, they too have become sinful in the eyes of God. Many people take only portions of God's Word and build them into doctrines without considering other portions that bring balance to the ones they are propagating. This always results in error as they have taken extreme views of God's Word. A great deal of division in the body of Christ is due to this very problem.

Those outside of the body of Christ are also affected as they see things within the church that should not exist and therefore want no part of Christianity because of these extremes. When people get out-of-balance in certain areas, it turns others away from Jesus instead of bringing them to Jesus. We have all been guilty of this at times, as it is not always easy to walk in perfect balance with the Lord.

However, the Holy Spirit's desire is that we learn this balanced walk as it is the only way we will come into perfection. When the Holy Spirit is doing something new, the pendulum sometimes does swing rather far in one direction as people are so eager to hear and practice new truths. However, after these are learned it is important that they swing back into balance or else they will end up in extremes that will bring discord into their lives.

Baptism of the Holy Spirit

A good example of this would be the past move of the Holy Spirit concerning "speaking in tongues." The church had practically lost the truth of the baptism in the Holy Spirit and speaking in tongues. The Pentecostals were virtually the only ones that were still carrying this "torch." Many people in the denominational church world had never heard about the beautiful gifts of the Holy Spirit. God saw the need for this beautiful truth to be restored to His entire church so He began pouring out His Holy Spirit upon all of His people regardless of their church affiliation, and many received and began "speaking in tongues" and "praising the Lord."

And it shall come to pass in the last days, saith God, I will pour out of my Spirit upon all flesh: and your sons and your daughters shall prophesy, and your young men shall see visions, and your old men shall dream dreams: And on my servants and on my handmaidens I will pour out in those days of my Spirit; and they shall prophesy (Acts 2:17-18).

Then Peter said unto them, Repent, and be baptized every one of you in the name of Jesus Christ for the remission of sins, and ye shall receive the gift of the Holy Ghost. For the promise is unto you, and to your children, and to all that are afar off, even as many as the Lord our God shall call (Acts 2:38-39).

While Peter yet spake these words, the Holy Ghost fell on all them which heard the word. And they of the circumcision which believed were astonished, as many as came with Peter, because that on the Gentiles also was poured out the gift of the Holy Ghost. For they heard them speak with tongues, and magnify God (Acts 10:44-46).

Peter prophesied that the baptism with the Holy Ghost (Holy Spirit) would be available to all believers in the last days.

Emphasis on the Giver, not the Gifts

The last days refer to the time between the first Advent (birth of Christ) and the Second Advent (the coming of Jesus to establish His kingdom). Therefore we are living in the last days. The first Advent has already occurred and He is coming soon to establish His reign. It is evident that the baptism in the Holy Spirit is being poured out today on all who will receive it. Many who are receiving are so overjoyed with this beautiful experience they begin to enthusiastically share it with others. In their enthusiasm many times "speaking in tongues" is stressed beyond what the Holy Spirit intends. This then puts too much emphasis on "speaking in tongues" instead of on the real gift of the Holy Spirit, which is being filled with His Presence.

This out-of-balance enphasis causes the gifts to become more important than the Giver. The Holy Spirit's presence is always more important than that of the evidence of that presence. We need both God's nature (love) and God's power (His gifts). We should stress neither to the point of being imbalanced. The Lord wants His entire church to enjoy all of His blessings and gifts. Instead, those who are gifted many times look down on those who do not know the blessings of Pentecost. On the other hand, those who haven't experienced the baptism in the Holy Spirit often view those who "speak in tongues" with distaste, especially when they have not sought the Lord in regard to this experience. The world of non-believers views a split and confused church. Generally the evangelical church today is categorized into three different groups: the Charismatics, the Pentecostals, and the Denominations.

Most outsiders view the Charismatic Movement as a group of people strangely carrying on with dancing, clapping and singing, with unusual gifts being manifested. Many physical healings and miracles are evidenced as the blessings of the physical man are stressed. The word charismatic is derived from the Greek word charizomai, which means primarily the "bestowing of God's gifts." Modern-day man has taken this word to mean anyone who is especially gifted with talents, personality, etc. The New Testament uses the word "charisma" and its derivatives approximately 400 times. Charismatics stress the physical manifestations of the gifts of God.

Falling Under the Power

Outsiders who look at the Pentecostals generally say that these people are too emotional as they cry, shout and fall down. (Hence, they have been called "Holy Rollers.") Since outsiders have no understanding of spiritual things, they do not realize that the phenomenon of "falling" under the power of God is Biblical.

The Pentecostals have long carried the torch of the baptism in the Holy Spirit with the accompanying manifestations of speaking in tongues and the "slaying power" of the Spirit. The Charismatics have now taken it forth, but for many years only the Pentecostals held on to these truths. They were faithful in spite of much persecution. Often people referred to them as "Holy Rollers" as part of that persecution.

What is the "slaying power" of the Holy Spirit that causes people to fall down? First, we should mention what it is not. It is not a blanket "badge of authority" when it occurs in someone's ministry. It is simply a manifestation of the Holy Spirit. God's power becomes so strong at times that it causes people to "fall down" under it. That is why it is commonly termed "falling under the Power," or another term used is "slain in the Spirit." This occurrence is recorded throughout the Bible and many people have experienced it.

Perhaps the most well-known Biblical account is the one of

4

Paul "falling down" at his conversion. **And as he journeyed, he came near Damascus: and suddenly there shined round about him a light from heaven: And he fell to the earth, and heard a voice saying unto him, Saul, Saul, why persecutest thou me? (Acts 9:3-4).** The purpose of this particular manifestation was to apprehend Paul so that the Lord could speak to Him.

John also had an experience of "falling down" under God's power when he was on the isle of Patmos. When Jesus appeared to him to give him His revelation, John could not stand up. **And when I saw him, I fell at his feet as dead. And he laid his right hand upon me, saying unto me, Fear not; I am the first and the last: I am he that liveth, and was dead; and, behold, I am alive for evermore, Amen; and have the keys of hell and of death (Revelation 1:17-18).** Jesus told John not to be fearful when this happened to him. Even so today we need not fear the power of the Holy Spirit as it is a life-giving Spirit. Many people today who "fall under" the Power are strengthened and receive instruction or revelation at the time, just as Paul and John did.

Another purpose of this manifestation is the power of protection. The Lord protected Jesus when the soldiers came to arrest Him. They did not take Him by force as they had planned, but Jesus went willingly. When they tried to force Him, we see God's "slaying power" causing all of the men to fall backward to the ground.

Judas then, having received a band of men and officers from the chief priests and Pharisees, cometh thither with lanterns and torches and weapons. Jesus therefore, knowing all things that should come upon him, went forth, and said unto them, Whom seek ye? They answered him, Jesus of Nazareth. Jesus saith unto them, I am he. And Judas also, which betrayed him, stood with them. As soon then as he had said unto them, I am he, they went backward, and fell to the ground (John 18:3-6).

Another time this phenomenon occurs is during worship. God's glory descends upon His people when they are praising and blessing Him. **And it came to pass, when the priests were come out of the holy place, that the cloud filled the house of the Lord, So that the priests could not stand to minister because of the cloud: for the glory of the Lord had filled the house of the Lord (1 Kings 8:10-11).**

Many people have received healing while "under the power" of God. God used this power as the first anesthetic when he took one of Adam's ribs to create woman from it. **And the Lord God caused a deep sleep to fall upon Adam, and he slept: and he took one of his ribs, and closed up the flesh instead thereof; And the rib, which the Lord God had taken from man, made he a woman, and brought her unto the man (Genesis 2:21-22).** There are other accounts of this "slaying power" throughout the Bible. **Matthew 28:4**, **Daniel 10:8-9** and **Matthew 17:6** are only some of them.

When this manifestation occurs it can be wrongly used if God's wisdom is not applied; that is why some are offended. We should be sensitive to the Holy Spirit when this happens and should not resist this manifestation, nor should it be exploited. If it is used as "a show" it certainly isn't under the Lord's leadership. Faith can produce this manifestation, and thus some ministers use it unwisely. (**1 Corinthians 13:2** talks about faith without love.) The Holy Spirit should always be in control; if He desires for this to happen then we should rejoice. However, if it does occur, it does not mean the Holy Spirit is not present. He manifests Himself in different ways at different times. Although the Pentecostals have borne the brunt of many verbal abuses due to this phenomenon, it still remains a beautiful blessing of the Holy Spirit. Anyone who has been "slain in the Holy Spirit" will testify to this fact.

Outsiders' View of the Church

Outsiders who enter Denominational churches usually perceive them as "dead" with programmed services that are geared solely to the intellect. They strive for good programs and good sermons. The intellect is being emphasized in most Denominational churches, the emotional aspect emphasized by the Pentecostals, while the Charismatics emphasize all the physical manifestations. Now we must remember we are looking at the church from the world's standpoint here in these statements, as we know not all Denominational churches, nor all Pentecostal churches, nor all Charismatics fit into these categories. Some individual churches of all groups are well balanced and truly Spirit led.

The Spirit of God is doing a new thing in these last hours; He is taking the emphasis off the churches per se and is putting it on the individual believers who make up the true church, which is Christ's body. The Holy Spirit is crossing all denominational boundaries and bringing His people together in unity. Since Jesus is coming back for a church that is holy and without blemish, He is now in the process of cleansing her. **That he might present it to himself a glorious church, not having spot, or wrinkle, or any such thing; but that it should be holy and without blemish (Ephesians 5:27).** The Holy Spirit is removing those things that are displeasing to Him and is giving glorious things to His people. He wants to minister to His people in every area so that they might become whole.

He did not create an out-of-balance church. He wants to minister to the intellect of man, as well as to the emotional and physical aspects. He wants to minister to every area of our lives--spirit, soul and body. Therefore, instead of Satan using the differences in our expressions of worship, we should learn to receive truth from one another and ask God to balance us out in all areas.

Expressions of the Holy Spirit

The Holy Spirit is a person, and as a person He expresses Himself in many different ways of worship. We should embrace all those that are truly expressions of His varied nature. Sometimes the joyous aspect of His nature is manifested and the people are inspired to clap, shout, dance and sing. At other times, the "mood of the Spirit" is one of awesome stillness. It is a holy quietness where we worship in silence before the Lord. The Spirit of God manifests as a gentle dove.

There are also times when the Holy Spirit demonstrates His heart of grief over a certain situation and the Spirit of travail descends upon all the people. As the Holy Spirit leads, they will weep and cry together over some burden or sin. The Holy Spirit does not manifest Himself in the same way each and every time. We need to learn to flow with the mood of the Spirit. Churches that do not allow the move of the Spirit are without the Spirit's guidance and therefore cannot possibly be pleasing to Him.

The Lord is attempting at this hour to lead His people into real and meaningful worship experiences. We should be sensitive in the Spirit and allow Him to direct our worship; we should avoid the tendency to become conformed to just one method. We should experience every one of the different aspects of the Holy Spirit and embrace His every mood. God wants us to come into balance so that we can experience all the beautiful ways of worshipping and learning of Him: in silence and awe, in clapping, dancing, shouting, lifting our hands in worship and praise, and in grieving when the occasion calls for it as God's heart reaches out to the lost and hurting.

We can learn God's ways and have our minds renewed through anointed teaching which ministers to our intellect. There is a time to clap, to dance, to weep, and to do all these varied things as the Holy Spirit directs. **A time to weep, and a time to laugh; a time to mourn, and a time to dance (Ecclesiastes 3:4).** We can corporately worship the Lord in many different ways. We will not have problems as long as there is unity and everyone is flowing within the Holy Spirit's desires. Our major problems arise when one member gets out of order and disharmony occurs. Paul wrote the Corinthians in regard to similar problems in their church **(1 Corinthians 14)**. The Holy Spirit desires to manifest

8

Himself in spite of those who get out of order because they have not yet learned to control their spirits. The Lord desires all of His varied moods to be experienced by the body of Christ.

The Lord is desiring to bring His body into unity while Satan is coming against them to divide and separate. If Satan doesn't use the differences in the way Christians worship to separate them, then He divides them in regard to various doctrines. Of course, certain doctrines are not Scriptural and to condone them would be agreeing with error. However, doctrinal differences should not separate members of the body. We can love those members who are in error until they come into the knowledge of the truth. As all Christians seek the truth, the Lord will expose those doctrines which are in error and will cause the truth to shine forth.

Water Baptism

A typical example of this is the basic doctrine of water baptism which calls for immersion instead of sprinkling. Many groups that have only sprinkled in times past are now seeing the Scriptural method is total immersion in water. In fact, the Greek word "baptism" means to immerse, submerse and emerge. Water baptism is an act of obedience that follows conversion to portray symbolically the washing away of our sins.

The baptism itself does not bring salvation; salvation inspires the water baptism. Those who have received Jesus in their hearts then desire to follow Him in this sacrament. Jesus Himself came to John the Baptist to receive His water baptism because He was to take the sins of the world at His death. These sins would be washed away by God for those who put their trust in Him. **The next day John seeth Jesus coming unto him, and saith, Behold the Lamb of God, which taketh away the sin of the world. This is he of whom I said, After me cometh a man which is preferred before me: for he was before me. And I knew him**

9

not: but that he should be made manifest to Israel, therefore am I come baptizing with water (John 1:29-31).

Anyone who receives water baptism must realize what it means to receive it; therefore, infant baptism is not Scriptural. One must repent and be saved to be baptized. Water baptism portrays the burial of the old man and his works of death and the raising out of the water into the new life in Christ. An infant cannot repent. However, parents can dedicate their babies to the Lord, as there are many accounts of this throughout the Bible. Hannah prayed a beautiful prayer when she dedicated her son Samuel to the Lord, **For this child I prayed; and the Lord hath given me my petition which I asked of him: Therefore also I have lent him to the Lord; as long as he liveth he shall be lent to the Lord (1 Samuel 1:27-28).** John's baptism of repentance was to prepare the way for the baptism of the Holy Ghost by Jesus.

I indeed baptize you with water unto repentance: but he that cometh after me is mightier than I, whose shoes I am not worthy to bear: he shall baptize you with the Holy Ghost, and with fire (Matthew 3:11). And John bare record, saying, I saw the Spirit descending from heaven like a dove, and it abode upon him. And I knew him not: but he that sent me to baptize with water, the same said unto me, Upon whom thou shalt see the Spirit descending, and remaining on him, the same is he which baptizeth with the Holy Ghost. And I saw, and bare record that this is the Son of God (John 1:32-34).

Baptism in the Holy Spirit

The baptism in the Holy Ghost is a crisis experience just as our initial conversion experience was. We cannot be gradually baptized in the Holy Spirit, just as we cannot be gradually baptized in water. Certainly we can be gradually filled with God's Spirit, but one day that "filling" will spill over into a baptism or complete immersion in the Holy Ghost. Many believe they need not ask for this experience because they think they receive the Holy Spirit at conversion. While this is true in the sense that the Holy Spirit comes upon us, and in us, to plant the seed of life in Christ, it is not true that we are completely filled with His Spirit unless we ask for it. **...How much more shall your heavenly Father give the Holy Spirit to them that ask him? (Luke 11:13).**

Many people have been "born again" and have the Holy Spirit working in their lives, but have never received the baptism in the Holy Ghost which equips them for service and gives them the power needed to overcome in Christ. **For John truly baptized with water; but ye shall be baptized with the Holy Ghost not many days hence...But ye shall receive power, after that the Holy Ghost is come upon you: and ye shall be witnesses unto me both in Jerusalem, and in all Judea, and in Samaria, and unto the uttermost part of the earth (Acts 1:5 and 8).** If you, as a Christian, have not known the power of God in being able to overcome sin, to witness and to know God in His fullness, then you need to ask God for the baptism in the Holy Ghost. There were also Christians in Paul's day who did not know about the power that was available to them. We find this recorded in **Acts 19:2-6,**

He said unto them, Have ye received the Holy Ghost since ye believed? And they said unto him, We have not so much as heard whether there be any Holy Ghost. And he said unto them, Unto what then were ye baptized? And they said, Unto John's baptism. Then said Paul, John verily baptized with the baptism of repentance, saying unto the people, that they should believe on him which should come after him, that is, on Christ Jesus. When they heard this, they were baptized in the name of the Lord Jesus. And when Paul had laid his hands upon them, the Holy Ghost came on them; and they spake with tongues, and prophesied.

This Scripture clearly shows us there is more than one baptism. These Christians had received water baptism, but not the Holy Ghost baptism until Paul laid his hands on them and prayed.

We also see that the gifts of the Holy Spirit accompany this baptism, as they spoke in tongues and prophesied.

Another account of this taking place is found in **Acts 8:14-20: Now when the apostles which were at Jerusalem heard that Samaria had received the word of God, they sent unto them Peter and John: Who, when they were come down, prayed for them, that they might receive the Holy Ghost: (For as yet he was fallen upon none of them: only they were baptized in the name of the Lord Jesus.) Then laid they their hands on them, and they received the Holy Ghost. And when Simon saw that through laying on of the apostles' hands the Holy Ghost was given, he offered them money, Saying, Give me also this power, that on whomsoever I lay hands, he may receive the Holy Ghost. But Peter said unto him, Thy money perish with thee, because thou hast thought that the gift of God may be purchased with money.**

Holy Spirit Is a Gift

Still again we find an account of the gift of the Holy Spirit being given in **Acts 11:14-17:**

Who shall tell thee words, whereby thou and all thy house shall be saved. And as I began to speak, the Holy Ghost fell on them, as on us at the beginning. Then remembered I the word of the Lord, how that he said, John indeed baptized with water; but ye shall be baptized with the Holy Ghost. For as much then as God gave them the like gift as he did unto us, who believed on the Lord Jesus Christ; what was I, that I could withstand God?

God's gift of the Holy Ghost is promised to us today and not just for the saints back then as we find Peter saying, **...Repent, and be baptized every one of you in the name of Jesus Christ for the remission of sins, and ye shall receive the gift of the Holy Ghost. For the promise is unto you, and to your chil-**

dren, and to all that are afar off, even as many as the Lord our God shall call (Acts 2:38-39). The Holy Ghost is God's gift to us. As we are baptized in His Spirit we will find that we will experience the gift of speaking in tongues, plus all the other gifts when needed, if we continue to follow Him (1 Corinthians 12, 13 and 14). These are God's gifts of power to enable us to accomplish the task to which we have been commissioned. Although the gift has been abused by many, we should not take lightly the Lord's words to us in John 7:37b-39:

...Jesus stood and cried, saying, If any man thirst, let him come unto me, and drink. He that believeth on me, as the scripture hath said, out of his belly shall flow rivers of living water. (But this spake he of the Spirit, which they that believe on him should receive: for the Holy Ghost was not yet given; because that Jesus was not yet glorified.)

Zeal Without Knowledge

A "Balanced Christian Walk" is something that each of us needs to strive to attain since our eagerness and zeal can create problems for us. The Scripture talks of this in Romans 10:2, For I bear them record that they have a zeal of God, but not according to knowledge. We need the zeal, yet it must be balanced according to the knowledge of God's Word. The Scripture says in Hosea 4:6a, My people are destroyed for lack of knowledge. Dangerous heresies, erroneous teachings and false doctrines can destroy God's people unless they have a complete knowledge of God's Word. Just memorizing a few Scriptures will not keep us from error. We must study the Word of God and apply it to our hearts if we are to remain free from error and extremes. John 15:7 says, If ye abide in me, and my words abide in you, ye shall ask what ye will, and it shall be done unto you. This is a powerful promise of God, but it is conditional as we notice two "ifs" in this Scripture. These are if His words are abiding in us, and if we are abiding in Him. He states we can ask anything and it will be done if these two things are existent in us.

In looking at this Scripture, we can deduce that if our prayers are not being answered, we either do not have God's complete Word abiding in us, or we are not fully abiding in Him. We would be receiving answers to all of our prayers if we had all of God's Word in us and we were completely controlled by the Holy Spirit.

The way for us to be overcomers and get our prayers answered 100 percent is to allow the Word of God to dwell in us and change us until we are conformed to the image of Jesus Christ. Then we would never pray for anything that would not be the will of God for we would know and obey the will of God. God's Word is His Will.

If we are not receiving the answers to our prayers, we need to allow the Word of God to change us. The Word of God never changes, and Jesus never changes; so if there is any changing to be done, it must be on our end.

For I am the Lord, I change not (Malachi 3:6a). Jesus Christ the same yesterday, and to day, and for ever (Hebrews 13:8).

Jesus is the Rock. He is solid and stable and will not change. For this reason we can trust Him and believe the Words He has spoken to us. If He said it, then that settles it. It is truth because He cannot lie. If He said it and we believe it, then faith in His Word will produce those things that are promised to us in the Bible.

Knowing only portions of the Word can cause us to become imbalanced. We must seek to know the whole truth and be completely surrendered to the will of God for us to be victorious and successful Christians.

Stressing one portion of God's Word will invariably produce prayer failures. This is the reason for many "faith" failures today. It is not so much people's lack of faith that fails to produce the answers they are seeking, but their failure to apply other portions of God's Word.

Parable of Baking a Cake

To illustrate this, let me share a little modern-day parable. Jesus used this method when teaching on many occasions as the people could understand spiritual truths when He related them to certain physical situations. Most people can understand the process of baking a cake, so I want to liken the method for receiving answers to a prayer, to baking a cake. Baking a cake is not a very complicated process in itself. The main requirement for success is to follow the recipe. In this parable we are going to liken the Word of God to the recipe and the finished cake to our answered prayers. If we bake a cake and get a cake failure, we do not blame the recipe, but rather go back to it to see where we have failed to follow it. If we pray and do not get our prayers answered, we should go back to the Word of God (the recipe) and see what ingredients we have omitted or wrongly measured.

There are certain conditions in the Word of God that must be met in order for our prayers to be answered. They are not met automatically. In preparing a cake, the ingredients must be measured out and put together correctly to produce the desired result. The same is true with the Word of God; it must be balanced to obtain the desired end. **Divers weights are an abomination unto the Lord; and a false balance is not good (Proverbs 20:23).** Without balance we run into problems in receiving the things of God that belong to us. Let us look at a few basic ingredients from God's Word that are necessary in order to receive our answers.

Ingredient: Claiming God's Word

The first ingredient we are going to put in the mixing bowl is Claiming the Word of God. Before we can receive anything from God, we must know the Scripture that pertains to our need and desire. If God's Word makes us any promises, then they are ours if we lay hold of them and claim them. Let us liken the claiming to the flour in our cake recipe. As we place the flour in a bowl, it is obvious that all we have is flour. We can claim and claim continuously, but without other ingredients we will never have success. God has raised up teachers who have shared with the body of Christ our rights in Him. They have been teaching about those blessings that belong to us as God's children.

So many of God's people have not known the blessings that are theirs. Healing is a perfect example of one blessing that has not been received because we did not know it was ours as children of God. Prosperity, protection and victory belong to us, but we must claim those blessings to receive them. Many Christians have not known the advantages they have in Christ, and thus have lived far below their privileges. We have inherited a vast fortune through Christ's death on the cross. He died that we might live. He came to give us life more abundantly. **I am come that they might have life, and that they might have it more abundantly (John 10:10b).**

When men die they leave a will. In that will they list the inheritance. The Bible is Jesus' last will and testament and is referred to as the Old and New Testament. The New Testament is the new covenant which not only includes all the Old Testament promises, but also gives us new ones that are even better.

Ye are the children of the prophets, and of the covenant which God made with our fathers, saying unto Abraham, And in thy seed shall all the kindreds of the earth be blessed (Acts 3:25). But now hath he obtained a more excellent ministry, by how much also he is the mediator of a better covenant, which was established upon better promises (Hebrews 8:6).

Realizing the precious promises that have been left to us, we then must claim them to become benefactors. When the devil whispers to us that these things are not for us, we must simply get the will (God's Testament) and declare what is written there. God's Word is true, and if He says we can be healed, then we can. If He says we get the blessings, then we do. If He says we can be over-comers, then we can. If He says we should prosper, then we can. If He says our children can be saved by our faith, then they can. If He says we are delivered from fear, then we are. If God's Word says it, that should settle any questions we may have about it. We get the blessings as children of the King; however, we must first claim them. **Yet ye have not, because ye ask not (James 4:2b).** Claiming alone, however, will not produce those blessings; we must add other ingredients from God's Word along with it.

Ingredient: Confession of the Mouth

When we bake a cake we add milk to the flour, so I want to liken this to the Confession of Our Mouth. Claiming alone is not enough; we must begin confessing what the Word of God has to say about our need. We need to clarify here that this kind of confession is not the so-called "positive confession" taught by the success propagators in the world. Their "positive confessions" are directed toward "self," not toward God's Word. They build their "castles in the sky," but they are not founded on the Word of God; instead they are based on what they desire for "self." For example, you will never hear them confessing the following portion of God's Word, **If we suffer, we shall also reign with him; if we deny him, he also will deny us (2 Timothy 2:12).**

In confessing God's Word, we must not pick out only the Scriptures we desire, but also the ones the Lord desires for us. He certainly desires to bless us, but He also desires to cleanse us. We must be as enthusiastic in our confessions to be cleansed from all that would offend the Lord as we are in confessing the physical blessings He has promised us. We must learn to set a guard on our mouths as it is very important to control our conversation. We will ultimately receive the things that we speak. If we speak evil long enough, it will come to pass; likewise if we speak good.

Whoso offereth praise glorifieth me: and to him that

ordereth his conversation aright will I shew the salvation of God (Psalm 50:23). A man's belly shall be satisfied with the fruit of his mouth; and with the increase of his lips shall he be filled. Death and life are in the power of the tongue: and they that love it shall eat the fruit thereof (Proverbs 18:20-21).

We must not only claim God's Word, but also learn to speak or confess His Word. We must confess our faith in God's Word.

We must not confess lack, as the Heavenly Father has given us everything we need. We must not confess defeat, as God has made us more than conquerors. We must not confess doubt, as God has given us His faith. We are to speak the things that the Word of God declares as truth. We easily quote what men have to say on a subject, and many times we believe them despite what the Word of God has to say about it. Yet we are often hesitant to quote what God says because the devil tells us we would be lying. He causes us to look at our circumstances rather than the Word. Circumstances are subject to change, and one of the things that can cause them to do so is the confession of God's Word over a particular situation.

For instance, if we are in need of finances, the devil will try to get us to confess such things as "I don't know where the money is coming from to pay this bill," or "I don't know what we will do when we can't make the house payment." Instead, we need to align our confession with the Word of God. **My God shall supply all your** (my) **need according to his riches in glory by Christ Jesus (Philippians 4:19) But seek ye first the kingdom of God, and his righteousness; and all these things shall be added unto you** (me) **(Matthew 6:33).** (Emphasis is mine). We should confess our faith and trust in the Lord by saying, "I don't know how the Lord is going to help us meet this need, but I confess that He will because He cares for us."

We bring evil and good things forth by what we speak. Jesus referred to this in **Matthew 12:34-37:**

O generation of vipers, how can ye, being evil, speak good things? for out of the abundance of the heart the mouth

speaketh. **A good man out of the good treasure of the heart bringeth forth good things: and an evil man out of the evil treasure bringeth forth evil things. But I say unto you, That every idle word that men shall speak, they shall give account thereof in the day of judgment. For by thy words thou shalt be justified, and by thy words thou shalt be condemned.** As Christians we should never again confess any of the things that are against God's Word. Let me share with you "My Never Again List" taken from Don Gossett's book, What You Say Is What You Get.

"My Never Again List"

Never again will I confess "I can't," for **I can do all things through Christ which strengtheneth me (Philippians 4:13)**.

Never again will I confess lack, for **My God shall supply all of my needs according to His riches in glory by Christ Jesus (Philippians 4:19)**. Never again will I confess fear, for **God hath not given us the spirit of fear; but of power, and of love, and of a sound mind (2 Timothy 1:7)**. Never again will I confess doubt and lack of faith, for **God hath dealt to every man the measure of faith (Romans 12:3)**.

Never again will I confess weakness, for **The Lord is the strength of my life (Psalm 27:1). The people that know their God shall be strong and do exploits (Daniel 11:32)**.

Never again will I confess supremacy of Satan over my life, for **Greater is He that is within me than he that is in the world (1 John 4:4)**. Never again will I confess defeat, for **God always causeth me to triumph in Christ Jesus (2 Corinthians 2:14)**.

Never again will I confess lack of wisdom, for **Christ Jesus is made unto me wisdom from God (1 Corinthians 1:30)**.

Never again will I confess sickness, for **With His stripes I am healed (Isaiah 53:5). Jesus Himself took my infirmities and bare my sickness (Matthew 8:17)**.

Never again will I confess worries and frustrations, for I am **Casting all my cares upon Him, who careth for me (1 Peter 5:7).** In Christ I am "care-free."

Never again will I confess bondage, for **Where the Spirit of the Lord is, there is liberty (2 Corinthians 3:17).**

Never again will I confess condemnation, for **There is therefore now no condemnation to them which are in Christ Jesus (Romans 8:1).** I am in Christ; therefore, I am free from condemnation.

Never again will I confess loneliness, Jesus said, **Lo, I am with you alway, even unto the end of the world (Matthew 28:20). I will never leave thee, nor forsake thee (Hebrews 13:5).**

Never again will I confess curses or bad luck, for **Christ hath redeemed us from the curse of the law, being made a curse for us...that the blessing of Abraham might come on the Gentiles through Jesus Christ; that we might receive the promise of the Spirit through faith (Galatians 3:13-14).** Never again will I confess discontent because **I have learned, in whatsoever state (circumstances) I am, therewith to be content (Philippians 4:11).** Never again will I confess unworthiness because **He hath made Him to be sin for us who knew no sin; that we might be made the righteousness of God in Him (2 Corinthians 5:21).**

The confession of our mouths will eventually bring forth the things we speak.

When we are baby Christians who have not yet learned this truth, God, in His grace, does not give us the things we confess or speak wrongly because they are not in accord with His will. We have not yet learned His will. He looks on our heart, and simply because we are desiring to do the will of the Father, He cancels those things that are not His will. Our hearts are speaking louder than our mouths. **Lord, who shall abide in thy tabernacle? who shall dwell in thy holy hill? He that walketh uprightly, and worketh righeousness, and speaketh the truth in his heart (Psalm 15:1-2).** If we continue to speak truth in our hearts, our

20

mouths will soon begin to line up with our hearts. However, until that time the Lord is gracious to us when our hearts and our mouths are not agreeing.

This is a perfect example of two agreeing before the answer to prayer can come to pass. My mouth and heart must agree to produce the answers to my prayers. **Again I say unto you, That if two of you shall agree on earth as touching any thing that they shall ask, it shall be done for them of my Father which is in heaven (Matthew 18:19).**

One area that tends to get out-of-balance in the "Confession Teaching" is the tendency to not allow others to speak, but continually to correct their negative confessions of speech. We must remember that the highest law is the law of love, and we should not nag at others, but pray for them. Of course, we can gently help correct those who have the same knowledge as we do, as they would usually be eager to overcome in this area. However, for those who have never heard, it would usually be wisdom to just pray for them until they come to the knowledge of the truth.

One other area that is often abused is claiming and confessing only material things. Many are heard claiming cars, property, houses, etc., but we seldom hear them claiming souls. We should be sure our priorities are right when claiming and confessing. The Lord's greatest desire is for us to grow in Him and to bring others to the knowledge of His love. When we are not stressing this in our confessions, we are being led astray by the devil.

Another area that gets pushed out-of-balance is to feel we must continually confess what we are believing before men. We begin telling everyone, everywhere we go, the things God has promised us. We should exercise wisdom, for many times it is not wise to do much speaking. We are not required to confess our promises to everyone for them to come to pass. In fact, the Word of God teaches prudence and wisdom in regard to our speaking. **A word fitly spoken is like apples of gold in pictures of silver (Proverbs 25:11). A fool uttereth all his mind: but a wise man keepeth it in till afterwards (Proverbs 29:11).** Our main confession should be unto the Lord. It also builds our own faith when we confess with our mouths the victory we have in Jesus. Prayer time should be our main time of confessing God's promises so that not only He can hear us, but also the devil will hear our words. Then, if our words are aligned with the Word of God, the devil must bow his knee to those words. We will find that our words have overcome the enemy.

Ingredient: Faith

We claim the promises in the Word of God, which is the flour of our cake, then we add the confession of our mouth, which is the milk. However, without other ingredients we still only have a paste. Let us add another important ingredient to our recipe, the baking powder. Let us call this Faith, because as faith rises in our hearts we will begin to see answers to our prayers. We can receive nothing from the Lord except by faith, as that is the means He has chosen. What is faith and how does it work?

Hebrews 11:1-3, Now faith is the substance of things hoped for, the evidence of things not seen. For by it the elders obtained a good report. Through faith we understand that the worlds were framed by the word of God, so that things which are seen were not made of things which do appear. The above verse states very plainly that faith is a reality, something that gives "substance" to things before they become visible to the natural eye. **2 Corinthians 5:7** declares that we walk by faith, not by sight. When we are "born again" we are given spiritual eyes to see things and understand things that otherwise we could not discern without the Holy Spirit. When we are submitted to the Lord, He then begins to guide and lead us by His Spirit; we follow Him in faith knowing He will not disappoint us or lead us astray. We must learn to obey Him even when we do not see or understand how He is leading.

The Word of God states, **Whatsoever is not of faith is**

sin (Romans 14:23b). Some people refer to the expression "blind faith," but our faith is not a blind faith; it is faith in a very real person, Jesus Christ. We were blind before our eyes were opened to His love and forgiveness, but now we see Him and a new life and world belong to us.

Romans 12:3b says, **God hath dealt to every man the measure of faith.** We are then to allow the Holy Spirit to move in our lives so that our faith might grow in Him. For faith to grow and for God to honor our faith there are several principles we must follow in the Word of God since faith alone cannot produce our prayer answers.

Romans 10:17 says, **So then faith cometh by hearing, and hearing by the word of God.** We must know the Word of God for our faith to increase. Many times, we take only a portion of His Word and quote it and expect answers, when we must learn other portions that work along with the portion we are quoting. An example would be if we do pray a prayer of faith, yet do not obey God, our faith would be in vain.

Let's look at **Hebrews 11:4** for an example of this: **By faith Abel offered unto God a more excellent sacrifice than Cain, by which he obtained witness that he was righteous, God testifying of His gifts: and by it he being dead yet speaketh.**

Why was God pleased with Abel and not with Cain? Cain's heart was not right before God, thus his works were evil therefore his offering was rejected.

Not as Cain, who was of that wicked one, and slew his brother. And wherefore slew he him? Because his own works were evil, and his brother's righteous (1 John 3:12). Today, many people are doing the same thing, yet expecting God to honor their faith.

God wants you and me to be faith men and women, so that we can have good success in all that we do. **Joshua 1:8** says, **This book of the law shall not depart out of thy mouth; but thou shalt meditate therein day and night, that thou mayest observe to do according to all that is written therein: for then**

thou shalt make thy way prosperous, and then thou shalt have good success.

Hebrews 11:6 says, **But without faith it is impossible to please him: for he that cometh to God must believe that he is, and that he is a rewarder of them that diligently seek him.** We can see by this verse that we cannot please God unless we walk by faith. The dictionary defines faith as (1) unquestioning belief, especially in God (2) complete trust or confidence (3) loyalty.

In looking at these definitions, we can take a test and see if we really are trusting God with our lives. *Test question number one:* Do we rebelliously question what God is doing in our lives? Do we ask God such questions as, "Lord, when are you going to do this thing in my life? How much longer am I going to have to wait for my answer? Why haven't you answered my prayers, God?" All of these questions, if posed rebelliously, are just the opposite of faith as they gender doubt and are questioning what God is doing in our lives. Also, we are referring to people in this test who have made a total commitment to God and are trying to walk in His will. If we have not surrendered to God, there are things that happen to us that are not His fault because we are in the devil's territory.

Test question number two: Do we completely trust God and have our confidence in Him to the degree that when we don't see our answer right away, we wait patiently instead of taking the matter into our own hands and doing it our own way? Do we have confidence in the Lord that He has everything under control, or do we worry and fret and let anxiety rob us of our day? If we trusted Him, we would believe His Word and not doubt His promises.

Test question number three: What about loyalty? Are we loyal to Him? We act sometimes as if God were against us instead of for us. For instance, when we have prayed and asked God for an answer to our prayers but have not received that answer yet, do we begin listening to the devil as he whispers these words to us, "God hasn't answered your prayers; He doesn't really care for

24

you. You know God has all power in heaven and earth so why doesn't He answer your prayers?" Instead of our being loyal and defending the Father, we end up many times agreeing with the devil by turning to God and saying, "Yes, God, why haven't You answered my prayers?" Our devotion to the Lord should be one of defending the heavenly Father with a statement to the enemy like this, "Satan, I don't know why God hasn't answered my prayers yet, but I do know one thing; He loves me and my answers are on the way. If anybody is hindering my answers, it's you, not my precious Father."

Real faith has all the above qualities of total confidence in God, and complete trust and unquestioning loyalty. Do we really have faith in God? In discussing faith we need to point out that it is not the quantity of faith that will accomplish the overcoming in our lives, but rather the quality. **...for verily I say unto you, If ye have faith as a grain of mustard seed, ye shall say unto this mountain, Remove hence to yonder place; and it shall remove; and nothing shall be impossible unto you (Matthew 17:20).** It is not the amount of faith we have but who our faith is centered in. Jesus is faith.

If we feel we do not have sufficient faith to remove our "mountain of difficulty," we can always ask the Lord for the "gift of faith." This gift is one of the provisions for those who are baptized with the Holy Spirit **(1 Corinthians 12:9).** The Lord did not leave us without the tools to overcome our lack of faith. We can simply ask God to give us the gift of faith we need for whatever problem we might have. As we are faithful to exercise our "measure of faith" that has been given to each of us, our faith will grow. Then we can believe God for greater things even without the gift of faith. However, if we need the gift, we can ask and the Lord will supply if our hearts are right.

Faith is not only a gift, but also a fruit of the Holy Spirit plus a part of our Christian armour; so we see the importance of it in our Christian walk **(Galatians 5:22)**. May we be spoken of as were the Christians at Thessalonica, **We are bound to thank**

God always for you, brethren, as it is meet, because that your faith groweth exceedingly, and the charity of every one of you all toward each other aboundeth; So that we ourselves glory in you in the churches of God for your patience and faith in all your persecutions and tribulations that ye endure (II Thessalonians 1:3-4). Faith will carry us through every trial and tribulation. Faith is really not that difficult. God made it easy. In essence, faith is just taking one more step with Jesus; it's believing God for one more hour, and because we do not give up on God, He comes through with our answers when we trust Him.

Ingredient: Obedience

We must obey when God speaks to us and not try to get God to accept our way of doing things. His ways are higher than our ways. Our precious Lord would never ask us to do anything that would not bring a blessing to our lives. Sometimes that blessing is not immediately seen; yet if we hold fast and continue to follow in His ways, we will discover He has a most beautiful plan for our lives. We must let the Lord work His patient nature into our lives and not always expect instant answers. This is difficult for us as we are living in an age in which everything is instant: instant coffee, instant tea, instant mashed potatoes, etc.

So we see one of the things that must accompany our faith is obedience, which Abel was an example of. In fact, obedience is the next ingredient we need to add to our bowl. We shall parallel obedience with eggs in our cake, as eggs cause the cake to "stick" together. Faith and works go together; the one is not complete without the other.

We know that faith without works is dead. **Even so faith, if it hath not works, is dead, being alone. Yea, a man may say, Thou hast faith, and I have works; shew me thy faith without thy works, and I will shew thee my faith by my works (James 2:17-18).** The works mentioned refer to the works of the Spirit, not works of the flesh. We can do many so-called good works and still not be pleasing to God for He looks upon the heart and not upon the outward appearance. We must obey from the heart and do those things that are pleasing to God.

Cain approached God with a sacrifice that was not acceptable because rebellion was in his heart; he didn't do the things God required as Abel did. Many times we pray for God to do certain things, but we are not willing to be the vessels that He uses to bring them about.

For example, we pray and ask God to save our relatives, yet we want the Lord to send someone else to them with the salvation message. We must be willing to be the one God uses to tell them of His love. In fact, for every prayer we pray, we must be willing to be the vessel that God uses to answer that prayer. The Lord may not always require it of us, but we must be willing. If we are praying that God meets someone's financial needs, then we must be willing to be the one who does it. If we are praying for God to provide a place for someone to stay, then we must be ready to open our house to that person. Whatever we pray, if it is possible for us to be the answer, then we must be willing for the Lord to use us. We must obey God, even if our flesh is resisting what the Lord would have us do. We must determine to follow and obey God regardless of the cost.

The Scripture says in **I Samuel 15:22, ...Hath the Lord as great delight in burnt offerings and sacrifices, as in obeying the voice of the Lord? Behold, to obey is better than sacrifice, and to hearken than the fat of rams.** We can pray long hours, fast, and sacrifice in many ways, yet if we do not obey it will all be in vain. That is why many do not see the answers to their prayers. They refuse to obey the things the Lord speaks to them. Obedience and faith go "hand in hand." They will not work separately. Works of the Spirit are those that are unctioned by God. All works of the flesh are futile. When the Bible speaks of faith without works being dead, it is speaking of those spiritual works inspired by God. They are the outcome of our faith and walk with God.

27

When we walk with God, we will do those works that are pleasing to Him.

Ingredient: Fellowship With God

Another man of faith that is mentioned in **Hebrews 11** is Enoch. Enoch is spoken of as a man who pleased God. Wouldn't that be wonderful to be referred to as a man who pleased God? What was it that caused Enoch to be pleasing to God? In Genesis, the Scripture says that Enoch walked with God. Here is another factor that causes faith to "stick" together, our walk with God or our fellowship with God. It is imperative to mix obedience and fellowship with faith to make it work. If our cake recipe called for an egg, we would not separate the egg and use only egg whites or only egg yokes, but the whole egg.

Faith can never produce anything without a fellowship with God. We fellowship with the Lord through many avenues: our continuous prayers, studying and meditating upon His word, fellowshipping with His people, etc. The most precious thing to the Lord is that sweet communion from our hearts as we talk and walk with Him. Sometimes we become involved in doing many things for the Lord, yet we forget to just talk to the Lord.

One thing we should never neglect is our quiet time with Him. He longs to fellowship with us. Here was a man named Enoch who loved God so much and longed to be with Him so much that one day by faith he just walked right into heaven with Him. Our work for the Lord could be so much more effective if we just spent that time alone with God talking to Him, loving Him and fellowshipping with Him. Then we could have access to the counsel of heaven in regard to the things we are believing God to answer for us. There would be no unexpected surprises the enemy could throw our way. The Lord would warn us of Satan's plans and show us how to overcome him through His plans. How wonderful it is to have God on our side. The Bible says, **If God be for us, who can be against us? (Romans 8:31b).**

Ingredient: Motives

The next ingredient we are going to place in our cake mixture is shortening. Let us call this our motives. We can claim, confess, have faith, be obedient and fellowship with God, yet still not have our prayers answered if our motives are not right. The heart attitude is of utmost importance to our Lord. He desires that our hearts be as His heart. When this is not the case, He is limited as to the things He can give us for we might wrongly use them. If our motives are not pure, we can hinder the Lord's work instead of furthering it. We must ask the Lord to purify our hearts and motives if we are to be entrusted with His power.

We even pray with wrong motives at times without realizing it. Christians who pray for their loved ones or co-workers to be saved do so many times only from a desire to be relieved from their persecution. The Lord wants us to have His love for the unlovely and pray that they might enjoy the same blessings we have in Him. When we pray simply because we want relief, we pray a selfish prayer from the wrong motive.

If we have resentment toward those who are making it unpleasant for us, we can ask the Lord to remove it and replace it with His love for them. That love will overcome their objections to Christianity. The Lord desires to use us to reach out and be the instruments to bring salvation to them. If we keep our hearts right and love them, the Lord will either save them, give us the victory to rise above the situation, remove them until they are ready to receive Him or remove us from the turmoil.

The reason many people do not get the victory over situations is that they continually ask God to change the other person, when many times they are the ones who need changing. When we ask God to change us and give us the victory, then we are well on the way to becoming an overcomer. We need to ask God for His divine perspective regarding our situations instead of viewing them, and those around us, through our own narrow, limited vision. If we see our lives and others from God's standpoint, we will be able to endure momentary suffering as we behold eternal victory in the end. **For our light affliction, which is but for a moment, worketh for us a far more exceeding and eternal weight of glory (2 Corinthians 4:17).**

We must check our motives and ask ourselves if we are praying selfishly or for the kingdom of God's sake. We must be willing to be used in whatever way the Lord sees fit. Are we willing to suffer in a difficult place for the Lord? Are we willing to experience a worldly failure if it would build us spiritually? We can never fail with Jesus. However, we must qualify what we mean by failure. Failure in the world's eyes is different from failure in the Lord's eyes. Many times the Lord must destroy or tear down things so He can rebuild them according to His perfect plan. **See, I have this day set thee over the nations and over the kingdoms, to root out, and to pull down, and to destroy, and to throw down, to build, and to plant (Jeremiah 1:10).**

How often we hold on to things that God is trying to get us to release just so He can give us something better. God wants us to let them die so He can resurrect them and bring life out of them. Instead, we continue to hold on to things that are "stinking." They should have been buried long ago, yet we hold on to them pleading for God to salvage them. These are spiritual deaths. We must die to those things we desire so that His desires can come forth. If we will but let them die and be buried, they will come up and bear much fruit. The seed that dies and goes down will produce many more seeds like it. The Lord does not want to deny us the seed; He just wants to bring forth the harvest instead of simply the one seed.

Our hearts need to be cleansed of every self-seeking motive that is impure. Only then can God answer our prayers to the fullest. So many Christians have missed the full message of the cross.

They desire to rule and reign with Christ, but have no realization that before that can come forth, they must first suffer with Christ. They are like the "silly doves" spoken about in Hosea. They are filled with pride and lust and have no heart. They do not know that their motives must be pure in order to receive God's highest intentions for them. **And the pride of Israel testifieth to his face: and they do not return to the Lord their God, nor seek him for all this. Ephraim also is like a silly dove without heart (Hosea 7:10-11a).**

So, a pure heart with right motives is necessary to produce prayer answers, along with the other ingredients of claiming, confessing, faith, obedience, and fellowshipping with God. **Let us draw near with a true heart in full assurance of faith, having our hearts sprinkled from an evil conscience, and our bodies washed with pure water. Let us hold fast the profession of our faith without wavering; (for he is faithful that promised;) (Hebrews 10:22-23).**

Ingredient: Wisdom

Still another ingredient we need to put into our cake is salt. Let us liken this to wisdom. We can do all of the other things we have mentioned and still not receive our answers if we do not use God's wisdom. Before we move in certain directions we need to ask, "Is this a wise thing to do?" The Lord does not by-pass our minds when He speaks to us to do something. In fact, He instructs us to "think soberly" **(Romans 12:3)**. If we would apply wisdom to our prayer life, we would certainly pray more effectively. If we, by faith, put on the mind of Christ and His wisdom when we are praying, we will have intelligent, deliberate thought behind our prayers. When we are wise in our prayer life, we will aim directly at the target and succeed.

If we feel we do not have wisdom, then we can ask for it because the Lord promises He will give it to all who ask. **If any of** you lack wisdom, let him ask of God, that giveth to all men liberally, and upbraideth not; and it shall be given him (James 1:5). The entire book of Proverbs is essentially a book of wisdom. Reading and meditating on this book can teach us the wisdom of God.

We must fully understand that the wisdom of God is different from the wisdom of this world.

Where is the wise? where is the scribe? where is the disputer of this world? hath not God made foolish the wisdom of this world? For after that in the wisdom of God the world by wisdom knew not God, it pleased God by the foolishness of preaching to save them that believe (1 Corinthians 1:20-21). But of him are ye in Christ Jesus, who of God is made unto us wisdom, and righteousness, and sanctification, and redemption (1 Corinthians 1:30).

Jesus is our source of wisdom, and as we look to Him and walk with Him, we shall have His wisdom in all things.

When we are new in Christ, we have not yet been cleansed from the wisdom of this world so God gives us access to the power of the Holy Ghost. When we have been filled, we receive all nine gifts of the Holy Spirit. The gifts are manifested as we have need of them. One of these gifts is the "word of wisdom." This gift gives us God's thoughts in regard to our different situations. God's wisdom is "thinking like Jesus." Until our minds have been completely renewed to the point that this is a reality, we are supplied with "the word of wisdom."

God's Word tells us how to discern worldly wisdom and His wisdom in **James 3:13-17,**

Who is a wise man and endued with knowledge among you? let him shew out of a good conversation his works with meekness of wisdom. But if ye have bitter envying and strife in your hearts, glory not, and lie not against the truth. This wisdom descendeth not from above, but is earthly, sensual, devilish. For where envying and strife is, there is confusion and every evil work. But the wisdom that is from above is

first pure, then peaceable, gentle, and easy to be entreated, full of mercy and good fruits, without partiality, and without hypocrisy.

We need only to check our prayer requests with this list to see if we are asking in accord with God's wisdom. Will our requests bring about purity, peace and gentleness? Is it with ease that we can ask for our requests? Do our prayers always show mercy to others? We should never pray for bad things to happen to people in order to teach them a lesson. We need to always pray for God to be merciful. Do we ask for the fruit of the Holy Spirit to come forth in our lives and the lives of those for whom we are praying? Are we without prejudice? Are we honest before God? This is God's wisdom and if we apply it, we shall find our prayer answers will come more readily. Our recipe is now nearly complete.

Ingredient: Praise

Another ingredient that is mandatory, if this recipe is going to taste like a cake, is sugar. Let us compare the sugar with praise. We should always have the attitude of praise and thanksgiving toward God in our hearts no matter what kind of trial or trouble we are going through. The Bible tells us in **1 Thessalonians 5:18, In everything give thanks: for this is the will of God in Christ Jesus concerning you**. Now let us notice the Scripture says to praise God in everything, not for everything. It is the will of God to always be thankful. Everything that happens to us is not always the will of God.

One of the first things we need to know about God is that He is the source of all good things. He loves us. In fact, the Scripture says He loved us so much He sent His son Jesus to die for us so that we might have life and have it more abundantly. We should not believe in praising God for tragedies, for sickness, for bad things, yet we should believe in praising Him in these circumstances. You see, the bad things did not come from God and we don't want to blame the Lord for something the devil sent. Our God is not the author of sickness, sin, tragedies, sorrow and heartache. The devil is the one who sends these things and then tries to get us to blame them on the Lord.

Some people have trouble believing this because of certain Old Testament Scriptures that seem to say God is sending those things. One of these is the verse in **Exodus 15:26** that says, **...If thou wilt diligently hearken to the voice of the Lord thy God, and wilt do that which is right in his sight, and wilt give ear to his commandments, and keep all his statutes, I will put none of these diseases upon thee, which I have brought upon the Egyptians: for I am the Lord that healeth thee.** Because of God's dealings with the Old Testament people in a sovereign way, they attributed both good and evil to the Lord. Most of the people did not know the Lord in a personal way so their gauge for pleasing the Lord was based on whether they were receiving what they believed to be God's blessings or curses.

God sent His prophets to tell them that it was their own fault they were not being blessed because they were sinning and not obeying Him. **Thine own wickedness shall correct thee, and thy backslidings shall reprove thee: know therefore and see that it is an evil thing and bitter, that thou hast forsaken the Lord thy God, and that my fear is not in thee, saith the Lord God of hosts (Jeremiah 2:19).**

The evil was not coming from God in a direct way; it was coming because of their evil and rebellion against God. **But they rebelled, and vexed his holy Spirit: therefore he was turned to be their enemy, and he fought against them (Isaiah 63:10).** God hates sin, and His judgment is always against it. He, however, loves the sinner and desires to bless him. If man refuses God's ways, then God has no choice but to destroy the sinner along with the sin. It is never His desire to do this for He wants all to repent and follow His ways.

Yet some people think God is not fair because He allows evil to exist. If He instantly destroyed all evil, man would be destroyed along with it. It is man's own evil ways that are responsible for evil, not God. **Yet ye say, The way of the Lord is not equal. O ye house of Israel, I will judge you every one after his ways (Ezekiel 33:20).**

It takes the Holy Spirit to give us understanding of many of the Scriptures in both the Old and New Testaments, and without His light some of the meanings sound ambiguous, contradictory, confusing, and even cruel and repulsive at times. The natural man cannot understand the things of God as it takes the Holy Spirit to interpret the Bible, for He was the one who inspired holy men of old to write it. **But the natural man receiveth not the things of the Spirit of God: for they are foolishness unto him: neither can he know them, because they are spiritually discerned (1 Corinthians 2:14).**

The Bible is a miracle of God. This work was written by many diverse individuals, living in widely scattered places, and separated by hundreds of years of time. Gathered together as a whole, it has become the best known and loved book of all time. Actually it is a collection of sixty-six books, thirty-nine of which are categorized as the Old Testament and twenty-seven as the New Testament. The Old Testament was written before Christ, and the New Testament after Christ's advent.

The Old Testament is more difficult to understand because it was written with God's truths concealed, while the New Testament was written to reveal. The Old Testament contained types and shadows of the things to come in the New Testament. Many Old Testament prophecies were fulfilled at the advent of Christ as this was one of the things that confirmed Jesus Christ to be the Messiah.

God is opening more and more of His truth to us by the Holy Spirit through His Word in these last days. One of these truths is the revelation of God's nature and purposes for His people. Many people are receiving healing, deliverance and miracles at this hour because of God's truth being revealed. Satan is being exposed and God's people are coming into their rightful inheritance **(Daniel 12:9-10).**

Many of us have fallen for the devil's lies in times past because we did not know what the Bible had to say about the nature of the Lord or the nature of Satan. Satan is referred to in the Bible as the robber, thief, deceiver, liar, destroyer and murderer. He is the one to blame for sickness, death and tragedy. God is the author of goodness, light, life, joy and health. When Jesus walked this earth He went around doing good and healing all who were sick. Yes, God does allow Satan to exist, but only until an appointed time, when he shall be cast into the lake of fire and all who do not know the Lord shall be sent with him.

The Lord did not leave us helpless. He made a way for us to overcome Satan through Jesus our Lord. Why are some Christians leading victorious, overcoming lives, while others are victims of the devil? It is because many do not know what the Word of God has to say about who we are in Christ Jesus and what we have been given. The Bible says we are joint heirs with Jesus and that Christ was sent so that we might destroy the works of the devil through Him.

If we belong to God, then the devil is off limits when he tries to bring sickness, poverty, sorrow, fear or any other bad thing; we can use the name of Jesus against him and he will flee. We can also use the weapon of praise, "praising God" no matter what Satan is trying to do to us, saying, "Lord, I love and worship You no matter what Satan is doing; I want You to know I love You, and Lord I know You love me." Satan will have to flee when we begin praising God because the Bible says the Lord inhabits the praises of His people. **But thou art holy, O thou that inhabitest the praises of Israel (Psalm 22:3).**

The book of Psalms is a wonderful book of praises and songs to the Lord. Some of the greatest Psalms of praises were written by David and recorded in **Psalms 29, 30, 34 and 103**. We can meditate on these words and find that praise will lift our hearts from despair.

Praise is one of the greatest weapons against fear and loneliness. Worshipful songs and music can lift us up when we are depressed or lonely. Praise can bring about our prayer answers for the Lord loves to fellowship with and give to those with grateful hearts. The Lord's nature is one of joy, and therefore He wants us to be joyful. We should be thankful and grateful for all He has done for us. His sacrifice for our sins on the cross should be enough to make us eternally grateful and cause us to praise Him for evermore!!

Ingredient: Fasting

In following our recipe we see it takes more than one ingredient to bake a cake, likewise in getting our prayers answered. If the Word of God is our recipe and the finished cake is likened to our answered prayers, the basic ingredients needed for getting our prayers answered are claiming, confession, faith, obedience, fellowshipping, motives, wisdom and praise. However, as with a cake that requires the basic ingredient but is made tastier by adding spice, so sometimes we need to add a dash of spice to our prayer life. Let us liken fasting to spice. A plain cake does not require any spice, just as our prayers can generally be answered without fasting. However, sometimes we need to add the ingredient of fasting, especially if we have done all else we know to do. This last ingredient can be just the thing needed to release our prayer answers.

The New Testament has much to say about this principle. Jesus told the disciples on one occasion when they were unable to cast a demon out of a child in **Matthew 17:21, Howbeit this kind goeth not out but by prayer and fasting.** The prayer and fasting here was to increase the disciples' faith because prior to this verse Jesus rebuked them for doubt and unbelief.

If we are tempted to doubt the Lord and our faith is attacked by the devil, one good way to restore our faith is by fasting and prayer; then we will have the faith to believe God for the things He has promised us in His Word.

There are several Scriptural methods of fasting.

Jesus, in the wilderness forty days and nights, went on a fast of no food, water only, as indicated by the Scripture in **Matthew 4:2** which says afterwards he was hungry, but not thirsty. The Lord will honor partial fasts such as fruit juices only, one meal a day, etc. The type and duration are not as important as the attitude of our hearts.

Motives should be checked closely when we are fasting about a situation. We should not fast to move the Hand of God, but rather to force the hand of Satan to release the thing he is trying to withhold from us.

Isaiah 58:6-9 says, **Is not this the fast that I have chosen? to loose the bands of wickedness, to undo the heavy burdens, and to let the oppressed go free, and that ye break every yoke?** We should fast with an attitude of selflessness, not with one of "what will this do for me," but one of "what will this do for others?"

Many people have the idea that they must go on fasts of days and weeks to receive the gifts and power of God into their lives. This is unnecessary as the gifts are free and the power resides within us **(I John 4:4b Greater is He that is in you, than he that is in the world).** These are manifested by our yieldedness and faith.

God does call some people on long fasts for certain reasons, but never one that would promote pride within. In fact, Jesus taught three things that should be done in secret: giving, praying and fasting. We should do these things as quietly as possible. (Sometimes it is not always possible to keep these things totally unknown; however, the real stress is put upon the attribute of humility while we are fasting.)

The Spirit of the Lord will speak to us in regard to the length of fast needed in a given situation as well as the type of fast, if we will but ask Him. The main thing is that we do it unto Him.

Patience and Endurance

Now if all the ingredients are mixed in the proper amounts and proper balance, we have a good batter. Let us pour the batter in the cake pan and place it in the oven. Now our part is done; we must wait for God to do His part. Sometimes this is the hardest part--the trial of patience and endurance. When we're put in the fiery furnace, immediately we want out; but it's God who's standing in the fiery furnace with us. He knows how to bake a cake and He won't let it burn. He's only perfecting our patience and endurance. We must let Him have His perfect work in us. **But let patience have her perfect work, that ye may be perfect and entire, wanting nothing (James 1:4).**

It takes time to bake a cake. It takes awhile from the time you sow a seed before you reap the crop. There's a growing period. God has a time and a season for every prayer to be answered. It would be rather ridiculous for us to go up to the oven and stand there for thirty minutes watching the cake bake. We could do other things. God has the timer set and when the timer goes off, it's His time. There's a time and a season for everything as it says in Ecclesiastes. We have our answered prayer when the cake comes out of the oven: Praise God! When God answers a prayer, it's always more than we ask for. When we leave it in His timing, He puts the icing on the cake. The icing is the overflow. We have a wonderful God. He doesn't stop with a plain cake; He puts the icing on it. We not only receive our answers, but in abundance so that we can share with others. Our baked cake will feed a party. Praise God!

Now let's check our recipe and see if we have all the ingredients.

Cake Recipe for Answered Prayer
(According to the Word of God)

Claiming	flour
Confession	milk or liquid
Faith	baking powder
Obedience and Fellowship	eggs
Motives	shortening
Wisdom	salt
Praise	sugar
Fasting	spice
Balance	or right amounts blending
Trial	in the furnace baking
Endurance and patience	timing
Answered prayer	finished cake
Overflow	icing
Sharing with others	party

We need to be encouraged, even if we have a cake failure. We needn't give up; we just need to check the recipe and start over again. If we keep adding and subtracting until we find the problem, we will eventually get our cake baked and our prayers answered. Obviously, we have covered only a small portion of God's Word in this parable. There are many other things that could be added. However, we can see that if we follow the recipe book (God's Word), we will eventually get our prayers answered. Some of them may come quickly, others may take years; but if we follow the Lord's leading and seek Him to correct our course, we will come out victorious. If we take a humble attitude before the Lord and allow Him to show us if we are out-of-balance in any area, then we will be successful.

"Father, we come to You in Jesus' most precious name, thanking You for Your love for us. Lord, You see the areas in our lives that are not in balance. We ask that You reveal those to us and help us to walk in the path of righteousness and Your holy balance. Deliver us from error and all that is an abomination to You.

Heal us today spirit, soul and body so that we might serve You by walking in a victorious Christian life. Let our lights shine so that truly others might see Your love in us. In Jesus' name we pray, Amen."

Index

Additional Books by the Author:

Book Titles in the OVERCOMING LIFE SERIES:

PROVE ALL THINGS
THE TRUE GOD
THE WILL OF GOD
KEYS TO THE KINGDOM
EXPOSING SATAN'S DEVICES
HEALING OF THE SPIRIT, SOUL & BODY
NEITHER MALE NOR FEMALE
EXTREMES OR BALANCE?
THE PATHWAY INTO THE OVERCOMER'S WALK

Book Titles in the END TIMES SERIES:

MARK OF GOD OR MARK OF THE BEAST
PERSONAL SPIRITUAL WARFARE

Christ Unlimited Ministries, Inc.
P.O. Box 850
Dewey, AZ 86327
U.S.A.
For online orders, please visit our website:
http://www.BibleResources.org

Postnote

The Millers are very glad to receive mail from their readers; however, they are unable to answer the letters personally due the volume of mail that they receive. They will be happy to pray along with their intercessors for all who write with a prayer request; although they do no outside counseling as they believe this should be directed to local pastors as outlined in Scripture.

Christ Unlimited Ministries, Inc. is a non-profit church 501(c) (3) corporation. All contributions are tax deductible. We appreciate your prayers, encouragement and support. Your purchase of this book makes it possible for us to share free copies of Bibles, teaching literature, tracts and downloadable audio/video materials with ministers in third world countries who would otherwise not be able to purchase them.

The Lord gave the word: great was the company of those that published it (Psalm 68:11).

For Additional Study

This book is taken from a course of Bible studies called the Overcoming Life Series. The entire series is a virtual "spiritual tool chest," as it covers a multitude of subjects every Christian faces in his walk with God. It also answers questions that many believers have concerning the current move of God. These are dealt with in a balanced approach and in the light of the Scripture. God's people are not to live frustrated, defeated lives, but rather they are to be victorious overcomers! Other books available with their companion workbooks are:

PROVE ALL THINGS - Christ warned that great deception would be one of the signs of the end times. In this book, instruction is given on how to recognize false prophets and teachings. Clear Scriptural guidelines are given on discerning the Spirit of truth versus the spirit of error. The book deals with how to judge without being judgmental.

THE TRUE GOD - This is a teaching on the character of God, explaining why God does certain things, and why it is against His nature to do other things. It differentiates between the things for which God is responsible and the things for which the devil is responsible. Our responsibility as Christians destined to overcome is made clear so that we can live victorious lives.

THE WILL OF GOD - This lesson teaches us not only how to know the will of God in our personal lives, family, ministry and finances, but also brings understanding as to why God allows sin, sickness and suffering in the world. As overcomers, Christians are not to suffer under many of the things we have accepted as normal.

KEYS TO THE KINGDOM - Instruction on how to gain authority in God's Kingdom through prayer is the topic of this book. Many principles and methods of prayer are covered, such as pray ing in the Spirit, fasting and prayer, travailing prayer, praise, intercession and spiritual warfare.

EXPOSING SATAN'S DEVICES - This book is a powerful expose' of Satan's tricks, tactics and lies. Cult and Occultic methods and groups are listed so Christians can detect their activity. Demon activity is discussed and deliverance and casting out demons is dealt with in detail. Satan's kingdom is uncovered and the Christian is taught to overcome through spiritual discernment and warfare.

HEALING OF THE SPIRIT, SOUL AND BODY - This book teaches how to overcome emotional problems, as well as physical ones, and how to receive divine healing. It also teaches how to renew the carnal mind and walk in the spirit of life, thereby overcoming depression, loneliness and fear.

NEITHER MALE NOR FEMALE - What is the woman's role in the church and home? Who is a woman's spiritual head and covering? Does God call women to the five-fold ministry? What does God's Word say about divorce, celibacy and choosing a marriage partner? These and other woman related topics are Scripturally examined.

EXTREMES OR BALANCE? - Many Christians have hurt the cause of Christ through "out-of-balance" teachings and demonstrations. This book shows how to avoid those areas. It also deals wisely with the excesses and extremes in the body of Christ.

THE PATHWAY INTO THE OVERCOMER'S WALK - This book contains answers to the questions an overcomer faces as he presses toward the prize of the high calling in Christ Jesus. How can we be conformed to the image of Christ? How does the Holy Spirit work with the overcomers in the end times? What are the overcomer's rewards?

PERSONAL SPIRITUAL WARFARE - Explains the invisible world of spiritual forces that influence our lives and how good can prevail over the evil around us as we prepare for the new kingdom age that is coming. This book will help you overcome problems in your finances, marriage, the emotional pressures of fear, anger and hurt. Here are the keys to victory through spiritual warfare.

MARK OF GOD OR MARK OF THE BEAST - Much has been written and said about the mark of the beast, but little has been said about the mark of God. What does the 666 mean and what is this mysterious mark? How is it linked to the world of finance? Has this mark already begun? This book answers many questions about the mark of the beast and the mark of God, and how they affect Christians.

Please visit our website for information on how to order the complete "Overcoming Life Bible Study Series." Our site is also an excellent source for additional books and Bible resources.

www.BibleResources.org

Purpose and Vision

Go ye therefore, and teach all nations, baptizing them in the name of the Father, and of the Son, and of the Holy Ghost: Teaching them to observe all things whatsoever I have commanded you: and, lo, I am with you alway, even unto the end of the world. Amen.

Matthew 28:19,20

Christ Unlimited is not "another denomination," sect, or just a separate group. It is an arm of the Body of Christ — the Church of Jesus Christ, which has been called to strengthen the Body at large. We also believe we have been called to help establish the Kingdom of God in the earth.

Christ Unlimited is involved with all Bible-believing Christians regardless of their church or denominational affiliations and committed to helping wherever possible in evangelistic and teaching outreaches.

Christ Unlimited believes that time is running out and the Gospel has not been preached to every creature. Many nations have not heard the Gospel, and in many places, doors for evangelism are closing. We believe it is time all Christians cooperated with the Lord in breaking down denominational walls for a united front line against the kingdom of darkness and in setting up the Kingdom of the Lord Jesus Christ by the power of the Holy Spirit.

Christ Unlimited provides such tools as to enable the saints of God to establish the Kingdom of God in the earth. We encourage groups of prayer warriors who will pray, fast, and intercede for the nations. This, we believe, is weapon number one. We teach believers how to overcome through spiritual warfare and through

51

knowing how to use their authority in Christ Jesus through the Word and the power of the Holy Spirit.

Christians need to know how to bring down the forces of darkness in their own lives and in the lives of those to whom they minister. We provide such tools as Bibles, literature, Christ Unlimited books and an online prayer ministry. We publish the Gospel going out via any means of communication, including the Internet, videos, as well as literature. We have teaching seminars, Bible schools, and correspondence courses, all aimed at winning souls to Christ and building the Body of Christ into maturity.

Bud and Betty Miller serve the Lord together as founders of the multi-visioned ministry outreach, Christ Unlimited. The outreaches of this ministry have stemmed from a tremendous desire to see the Word of God taught in its balanced entirety. The Millers are firm believers in prayer and, through prayer, have seen many released from the bondages of fear, failure, and defeat.

The outreaches of Christ Unlimited are in obedience to the words of our Lord in **Mark 16:15**: **Go ye into all the world and preach the gospel to every creature.** This mandate from the Lord presents a challenge to our generation as an estimated 25 percent of the world's population still have not heard the Good News of Jesus Christ.

Christ Unlimited Ministries also is dedicated to teaching God's Word. **Hosea 4:6** says: **My people are destroyed for lack of knowledge.** Many Christians are leading defeated lives simply because they do not know God's Word in its fullest.

Christ Unlimited Ministries has provided for those who desire to know God's Word in a greater way. The main thrust of the teaching and literature is directed at "How to be an overcomer." In the endtimes, we must be prepared to overcome the onslaughts of Satan. Many Christians are suffering needlessly, because they do not know how to overcome sickness, depression, divorce, fear, and financial failure. Christ Unlimited Ministries provides answers for troubled families as well as trains workers for service.

www.ingramcontent.com/pod-product-compliance
Lightning Source LLC
Chambersburg PA
CBHW020952030426
42339CB00004B/58